Without Warning
Tim Greenup

Published by Scablands Books
scablandsbooks.org

ISBN-10: 0-9907525-3-4
ISBN-13: 978-0-9907525-3-0

Managing Editor: Sharma Shields
Editor: Maya Jewell Zeller
Cover art and book design: Keely Honeywell

Printed in Spokane, WA by Gray Dog Press

Contents

1.

2.

3.

Cradle Song

Our outer flank was exposed.
From the north, where Titans grow and
fire crackles endlessly, screams heard repeatedly!
We'd been warned of a coming storm but
how little we knew of ominous tones. . .
The provisions devoured in hours! And a little boy
made to watch his mother burn alive.
Have you been to the outer rim where grass gathers?
he'd mutter into the cellar air.
Have you been to the outer rim where grass gathers?
That was the night I forced Matt to borrow a monster movie.
That was the night the snake beneath the bed quit trying.
That was the night her face finally faded and something new came in.
Have you been to the outer rim where grass gathers?
Have you felt the ground gather beneath you?
Repeatedly!

The Guys

So it's me, Tony, Chris, Brian, Neil, and Danny. And we're all in a cloud of
cigar smoke and whiskey fumes in an unfinished basement, talking about
women. Specifically, what it would be like to have sex with two of them
at the same time. We all agree that it'd be fun, but no one wants to try it
on account of all the legs. Four legs is a lot of legs to navigate
even on a king sized bed. So Brian says something about finding
some bitches without any legs. We all laugh until we stop laughing

and the basement gets quiet and we all go for one of Tony's éclairs.
These are exceptional, I say. Everyone nods, goes *mmmm*, and scratches
their beards. Neil turns on some surf music and brings up the new action
movie coming out this summer. Says the effects budget was in the trillions,
says it took some coaxing but Hans Zimmer finally agreed to score.
But no one else has heard of it, so Neil's monologue peters out
and we're stuck again staring quietly at the ceramic platter of pastries.

And then we hear a rustling upstairs — a dog barks, floorboards bend,
the basement door opens, and Terry comes barreling down the steps.
He's wheezing once he reaches the bottom. And Danny says, Jesus,
is that your breathing or did someone let the helium out of a balloon?
So Terry says something about fucking Danny's mother, sister, dog,
and girlfriend and we all start laughing, each strained voice straining
to drown out the others. A heap of pink panties drops from the ceiling.

1991

Inside the family house
it was Christmas. Mother was shredding meat.
Father and sister were asleep somewhere.
I opened the Yellow Pages to toxic waste distributors.
The vat arrived quietly on a flatbed truck.
Using a garden hose, I filled the attic,
thinking ooze would run down the walls
and make everything dangerous and more interesting.
How surprising. Father had caulked every crack,
sealed all windows and doors.
From the kitchen, he screamed,

For years I have yearned
to melt my son. Here!
In my own house!
Let's celebrate!

The Realization

Neighborhood graying from change.
Crows lift confidently
onto power lines and call
familiar names. In a far window,
a cat grows angry.
All that movement and defiance,
others are bound to be intrigued
and join in. And what then?
If all take to the sky, poor terror
gets bored, lonely, and dies.
And what then?

Smear Campaign

It was early morning, still dark, a Sunday,
when mother handed me a wicker basket
and sent me to the berry fields
to collect any blues, blacks, straws, or rasps
my tired eyes could see.

Her plan was to bake a pie,
I believe, and take that pie to village square
for the yearly Pig Belly Picnic.
There'd be dancing, mandolins, the women
in linen skirts, the children chasing
frogs across cobblestone, their
clodhoppers clomping
out into the green hills, while men
would crowd the keg, guzzling ale,
and speak of iron, of industry.

But when I returned, my basket full of berries,
black smoke billowed — cottages and floribunda ablaze.
The men held severed heads
by tufts of hair and chugged blood from the necks.
These men smelled of ham.

I dropped the basket and made for home.
When I spotted mother under
a mound of mortar and stone, the concerto began.
Piano, then cello, then
the French Horn and violin. I ran to her side
to brush away the rubble. Her lips were purple,
but breath still there. Between coughings
she said,
Freemasons, son. It was the Freemasons.

Oh, those Saturday nights,

rushing home from church and gliding into the T.V.
All of us — father, mother, daughter, and boy —
cradled by Hollywood warmth, a pizza delivery.
Other worlds swelled and splattered, coloring our eyes.

Then, late one year, tumbleweeds
crossed the kitchen
and hair filled the drains.
Mother was vomiting and shrinking.

Unsure how to proceed, we watched
from the Buick's backseat as
Dutch elm disease devoured the neighborhood
and Mother's face continued collapsing.

A Scene

The horizontal woman moves
into me. The ceiling dips and
presses our bodies, draining
them, like tofu on a countertop.
The mattress sops. We cannot
stop crying but keep breathing.
We're in a bad way. Over the hill
the castle waits for the fog
to take it back. A groundskeeper
outside the cemetery gates hears
a sudden hollow moaning.

July

Sun sets pink on suburban roofs.
Her cigarette smoke plumes luxurious.
I am eighteen and between puffs my girlfriend
realizes that she contains multitudes
and, therefore, can no longer see me.
I break mirrors for months.
I go on a safari and find myself
shuddering in a tree, covering
my penis with leaves. Below, some
predators sniff the air. There's an
alley in my chest that's clogged
with soil and ash. Once a fountain
glittered there, inviting reflections
of everyone I love into the world.
The ether streamed to my feet
to slosh while I slept. Dear,
when was this wrong turning
into darkness? My fingers tense;
I imagine a large garden calls
to exhaust them. Waves smash
into rocks. A lighthouse slips
into the sea. I am very sleepy.
Aren't you, Starlight? All that
glowing must be exhausting.

Sensing Human Hands Have Touched Her Baby, the Mother Bird Rejects It

One afternoon, I forget
my Necronomicon on a picnic table
somewhere outside Dubuque Iowa

before reentering the black
passageway beneath
the hills and bean fields.

Pouring, shaking,
a scratch, a pinhead of light
drops, and the corridor heaves

flame, driving me back to the bright
surface to retrieve something . . .
So strong the sun today, bleaching everything.

I wander dusty streets.
A man in mirrored sunglasses drives
beside me, slowly, watching.

You get away from that boy!
a husky woman shouts from a drugstore
doorway and the El Camino speeds off.

Come get some fresh sun tea, son,
she says, drying her hands
on her floral apron.

The store shelves are crowded
with cloudy jars, floorboards warped
and bloodstained. No sun tea yet, but

she has me chained to a chair and
drills are whirring right behind me. Oh, ouch!
Sharp black passageways!

At the Park

A pale boy holds a flower in his teeth
and makes shapes in the clouds — a candle,
the flame, an elephant searching for reason
in an unknowable universe. And the boy

thinks to himself, I deserve this respite
of bird call, warm grass, families walking past
in church clothes, though they haven't gone in years,
though they sometimes pray alone at night. He uncrosses

his legs and stretches. He rubs the grass with his hands,
breathes evenly and deeply. He knows he is here,
peering into the sun, though he is also wandering
the many tools of his father's musty garage

wondering what does what. He's always there
somewhere with bread crust by the duck pond
while a tall tree reaches out
and greens the water for centuries.

The Unruly Pond

At night black water
fills the bed
with snapping turtles.

The cat fights them
and is quickly shredded.
Beneath me

my deaf brother
finally sleeps.
Father opens the door,

dumps leeches everywhere,
and leaves, muttering,
it wasn't a dream

it was a flood
it wasn't a dream.
Nothing good ever crawled

from the woods
to hide under the deck.
Until mother arrives,

wielding flashlight
or flamethrower,
I reach for the knife, but

my fingers become snakes
and slowly wrap around
my brother,

still sleeping,
silent, stoic, and
covered in scales.

Things They Say

Someday it will be you, trapped
inside rows and rows
of cornstalks. You will be the one
cautioned about razor husks —
don't touch, don't you ever.

Cars pass. Colors flash.
Those are nothing, they tell you, just
animals lurking the perimeter.
You are safe here with us.
Why don't you stay? There are stories

some nights of a man who
made it through the cornstalks, past
the circling beasts. He went
as far as anyone could, they say, and ended
with a belly full of blackness
and a bloody, filthy mouth. That's all.
That's all he ever found.

Vanity Fair

How could she do this? Running off with another man and marrying him before she even meets me? I reject this impossibility. Chip away at it. Smile and begin dressing better (all around), correctly. A friend once told me, stop being so self-effacing. I did. My head got big. Chest and muscles too. I grew tall as trees — I was walking through the park at the time. Police and paramedics arrived, strapped me to a flatbed truck and drove to a distant countryside. Rolling me into the dirt, they insulted my body, face, education, and mother. Every pore whistled and sprayed heat. I was shrinking; I felt so insignificant; the only witnesses to my life were silent prairie grasses. Why shouldn't the ants carry me away? The medics needed to consult my manual but couldn't find it. Meanwhile, I toured the colony, met the queen, every ant chanting, He is king! He is king! How flattering! Instantly, my body expanded and tore upward through the dirt, fast as flames, the medics hugging me and crying, you rotten piece of shit!

The River

I wake beneath an overturned canoe.
It's late afternoon.
A skunk crosses the field.

A truck nears, revving.
Bullfrogs pack the river,
soaking up muck.

From the truck, dogs bark at the tree line.
The sun is brick red and angry.
Somewhere a hawk shrieks.

Men are approaching.
Mites pry into my neck and armpits.
The men whistle through reptilian lips.

They sit on the canoe.
They light cigarettes,
sneeze, and speak:

As boys we'd come here.
As boys we'd kiss.
Early morning birds
trilling and optimistic.

We meant to build sanctuary.
We pounded the trees.
Grubs fell from the leaves
and bored into us.

We were called home for supper.
We cut potatoes,
finished our milk,
kissed mother and were dismissed.

All the neighbors gathered
on the far hill hoping.

Moonlight came,
the stars falling
into the river and detonating.

We followed and
drifted to other counties.

Reeds collared our wrists.
Fireflies rose from the fields
and mud filled our mouths.

We twisted each other.
Glowing, we licked and
we kissed.

Somewhere our mothers
missed us.

The river was winning.

Parting the Ice Floes

I nap in a hammock
near the dying stream
of boyhood. My pale hands
tremble, for I am

a walleye in cold waters, sneezing,
eyeglasses askew. The
bottle empty
on the lodge floor,

bearskin rug still breathes . . .
The once deafening snowfall
ceases and a full-breasted Nordic woman
sings, parting the ice floes.

My bloated body
turns to face the starlight,
seeing instead my mother
as a young girl one autumn

in Minnesota, a lock of blonde hair
tucked behind her ear
while she walks alone
amongst the willows.

That Teenage Feeling

       Friends, nothing's funny about today.
I am bedridden by a pimpled face,
my trajectory uncertain.
       Hope puffs from my sweat-stained mattress.
Guitar solos fumble and fail and,
occasionally, coach yells
to take the field. I trudge out,
palms itching, rubbing
wallpaper in my neighbor's bedroom
closet while he strangles me with a belt.
       I climb into a treehouse
where my lips aren't too big
to trumpet, sing, or breathe.
       The neighborhood punk
sells me a baggie of oregano, claiming
it's weed; I push him against a wall
and squeeze his throat until he blacks out
and begins shaking
       the ice from his brain:
everyone's calling his name from the sandpit
of temporary kingdoms — the urine-moat
needs more rafts of hair.

The Encounter

Outside the downtown
haunted house, I waffle,
should I ask
for my 16 dollars back?

But Terry seems pleased,
so we check our phones
exhaustively for messages
and walk toward the bar.

Silhouettes
of young men head our
direction, coming
through the alley, onto Main,

but their bodies aren't brightening
beneath the streetlights. They stop
six feet ahead of us. We
step toward them, they

step back. We back away,
and they step forward.
Hmph, Terry says, decidedly.
The forms turn,

their mouthless faces move
closer and begin mashing together.
They violently embrace, hands
tearing at dark shapes.

The one ahead of me gracefully
kneels into an oily puddle and
unbuckles the other's belt.
Dude! Terry's clutching my arm,

let's go. We hurry to the bar,
where Michelle and Megan wait.

Both are beautiful, funny,
but I make miserable conversation.
I'm somewhere else entirely.

The Shower Ceremony

Kneel.
Close your eyes.
See something
you remember?
The old house,
your bedroom,
it's all
playing out now,
on the far side of your eyes.
Except this time the bed's
inside a railcar, tearing
through moonlight
toward a lake.
The conductor calls
faintly from some depth
that the doors
are closing. When
the train breaks water
there is no sound,
just a pounding
from the bridge
of your nose.

The Nursery

They stuffed my mouth with cake.
They fanned me and would
cry when I was troubled.
At night, I would think of them
climbing into a bubble bath.
I was the cherub glued
to the mirror's edge,
rotund face unimposing
but available. When I was good,
they touched me. Spanish guitar
trickled from the stereo like rainfall.
I dreamed of draining
their breasts, of becoming
the water on their thighs,
the towel drinking their hair,
the bed, shaping myself
around them, or the moon
in a nearby window lighting
the wind to prick their skin.

The Final Fantasy

Julie puts on her goblin mask for me
then slips off my pants.

Fade to black.

A pizza man thumbs
the apartment buzzer, and
I answer wearing only a lobster bib,
my fingers dripping.

Cue voice-over: How did things get this way?
Is it possible for me to change?
How did things get this way?

In real time: Julie's eating
the dream house,
pepperoni and cheese
smeared across
the sheets, lights out
with her computer
on my pillow
streaming reality TV.

I'm in the basement
in the bathtub with Puccini.
He's muffled by bubbles,
candles and waves,
urging escape.
I hold him under
till the music stops.

Spokane WA, Fall

I miss my friend Brent from Southern California. I planned never to miss anything from Southern California. Yet, here I am, at our coffee shop, watching the door. The door is an image that crops up often in dreams of those who feel, for one reason or another, trapped in life. There's life, Tim, says the gypsy dishwasher of the fried chicken restaurant I work when I'm sixteen, and then there's life! He tugs at his crotch. Somewhere surgeons botch a surgery, minnows swim blindly into the mouth of something ugly. On my bed, sixteen again, I listen to terrible choruses. I dig in my belly button for films or cheeses. Finger smells of something – crematorium, Gorgonzola. Forests of eyebrows fighting vainly against the flames. A tattoo inside my forearm I didn't ask for. After walking around outside all night, I return home and find my torso steaming, my feet cold but strangely sweating. Mother's going to be so mad at me.

We Need to Talk

Terry and I need a break.
We drive west for days.
An Agricultural Inspector at the
state line pulls us aside and says:

You Nebraska boys
ain't smugglin'
no despair into this state
of California, is ya?

Both thumbs tucked
firmly between the straps
of his yellowed overalls, his
immense pink and pimpled
forehead furrows and sweats.

No sir! we say, our voices
emphatic and in perfect harmony.

Wellll, go on ahead, then.

He nods toward the sun
and grins, suddenly handsome
beyond belief.

Me and my men
will be seizing your car, he says.

So it goes! says Terry and
throws him the keys.

Our calves convulse
and skip through a turnstile
into the desert.

We reach the coast
and stop skipping.

A series of scarlet
flashes. The palms
become ash. Every
beached body burns.

In a gasp between
laughters, a beeping
from my pocket.

Oh! I say. My phone! Almost forgot!
A message! From . . . Julie . . . she says
we need to talk.

Closing Remarks

When the ceiling fan breaks free,
who will it julienne first – me? Or the cat?

He never wakes me anymore.
No mewing.
No whispers in my ear
at 4 a.m. Hush hush, dear
master, it's all in your head.
No one to explain why
that isn't worse.

He's somewhere else
licking his asshole.

The day we lost our footing
I was popping spiders
with Kleenexed fingers.
The spiders had gushed
up through the floorboards.

He ran out the bedroom door,
took a corner and peeked back in.

Isn't this your fucking job? I said.

And the shouts began.
We digressed to
futures. We exhausted
ourselves silent.

After the local man was stabbed to death
by his wife, she torched him in his car
along with the entire wheat field.
No one knew what to say.

That blackened skeleton. The melted
steering wheel.

His quiet
throat full
of mews.

Becoming Jeff Lebowski, Edward Blake, Super Mario, and a Heap of Ash

Drowning vodka
with milk and mocha, we
bowl on the Asiatic rug. We
impregnate pale, red eyed women.
It's a life. We cherish it but
never forget the Germans —
techno music and grandeur looming.
Who knows what they'll do?
The Rapture happened.
Airplanes crashed
into the East; we wait
for the sky to split and
dump ash on everything.
One more reason to eat a burger
while watching pornography. Outside, everyone
wears sandwich boards, faces greased,
hollering *Nigh! Nigh! The End is Nigh!*
From rooftops, gargoyles
wash the city.
Below, some kid
gathers every gold coin,
walks to the fridge, steps inside
and immolates.

Drinking and Becalmed, Friday

A sudden wind tore
open the basement door. I approached, cautiously,
and called Terry's name.

Something shifted in a far corner, but
nothing came into the light.
I closed the door and sank, whimpering.

For the longest time, there'd been
something there. But never, anymore,
comes he, does he, offering advice

or sharp witticisms about life.
He'd always say, just start
kissing and go from there!

A Song for Everybody

By now everybody is sleeping
on a mattress somebody else died on.
So it goes. I've always said
the only thing you need in life
is a good Thermos or microwave
to keep your soup warm,
so you can sip it slowly
and watch everyone else
eat each other alive.

Of course, I speak from a place of privilege.
Most days people hear my name
and they cannot stop their fluids.
I am a wall cloud of sensation,
quivering legs and inducing stains
simply by waking.

If you ever thought you thought a thought
no one has ever thought before,
think again, and read my book.
It's all covered there. It's a calm song:
listen. And be saved.

A Loud Song Remembered Fondly

The bone splits the marrow
swallowed by dusty fields,

and I spend a weekend eating nothing
but beans.

When all the friends dart to different corners,
the middle hollows out.

Fill with beer
and shredded cheese.

Photos of the pale queen persist,
despite being boxed and burned.

The underground stream turns
toxic and begins bubbling.

All the bellies swell
with disease.

Remember the crown she proudly wore?
It drips now down her scattered face.

Before You Wake, Crying

You meet in the foyer of the mall
department store where she works part time,
weekends, so you can go to school to write
poems about shitty girlfriends. It is afternoon,

the Nebraska sun creeps closer to
your discomfort. You are nervous. You know
she is gone, but you cannot remind her.
Not now. She seems so strangely happy here

talking with her eldest son again, about nothing
dire. How good she looks
in those new boots. How you wish, for once,
to buy her lunch at the food court.

What couldn't you say
beneath those plastic palms?
Chlorine from the ground floor
wishing fountain wafting.

But, I'm sorry.

I can't, she says.
My break's just about over, honey.
Sometimes things are just about
like that.

The Pitfalls of Scottish Ancestry

Radiators start creaking.
I slip into a wool sweater
and boil roasts for hours. At once,
all the windows frost over.

The place fills with blue steam,
staining the walls, and soon the room's
a swimming pool, then it's a sea,

and soon it's a new home.
There's so much wrinkling and
lung strain, but it's not
terribly lonely. Still,

I'll grow some dolphins, then
Japanese fishermen will move in
with coy country daughters.

I'll be the mystery. Me and my
secrets snickering behind delicate hands.
They can't keep their eyes off

my inch-wide pores, can't not wonder
about the ruddy bramble of pubis,
my traditional, spineless grace.

Exterior: Night. Forest's Edge.

The woman wears a gold coat.
She touches your hand, then
runs deep between the slowly
shifting trees.
The leaves project her voice
in stereo, begging you to approach
and kneel,

to crawl inside
and rest

and wake to the two of you
at your favorite downtown
diner, pancakes
big as your head.
With a crayon you trek
the menu's maze
together.

In the twisting
hall of hedges, time stops.
All clothes peeled off, her
thrown coat becomes
the moss of this
other green world.

But first, she echoes
from the many dark trunks,
you have to find me,
and I never stop moving
and I never get scared
and there are so many like you,
yelping alone in the night.

Date Night

Sylvia and I had only been together two weeks
when she asked me to attend a women's rights rally
downtown. I really liked her, so I said I'd go.

On our way home, a man walking in front of us
turned around and said, hey man,
you nabbed yourself a real beauty there.

Congratulations and keep her close.
Sylvia snickered a little, then hugged me and held on.
Thank you, I said. Oh thanks so much!

Her magnificence reflects my value as a human man.
I squirmed out of her arms and rolled
up my sleeves. Easy there, the man began,

I was just trying to pay you two a compliment;
I wasn't trying to be a creep.
I swung at him.

He fell backward into an alley and hit his head
on a rusting grease trap. The smell reminded Sylvia of food.
Do you want to grab some dinner? she said.

Sure, I said, and pushed her to the opposite end
of the sidewalk. That would make for a delightful
evening. And this time, Sylvia, you're buying!

The Realest Place on Earth

Inside the antique shop we
found an oil painting of blank
human faces lapping up a red river.
A dark haze green and beyond
the hills crept forward. Well, well, well,

said the trench-coated silhouette in the corner,
cigarette smoke swirling.
Six bowls of ice cream later, we clomped
arm in arm to the farmers market
for some dates, which was charming,

almost exhausting. All those sharp, tight grins,
clenching the afternoon away.
My wife was attracted to me then.
Every hour a plant outside town dumped
bodies into the water,

mounds of them in nets
weighed down on all sides by bricks.
The thick lips of a tuna plucks a patch of skin
from a gray forehead, hair aflutter,
milky eyes open hollowly.

In some ways, it was the realest place on earth.
Threat of disruption always in the air, a wave
rising from the shore to wash the streets
with the dead, our schnauzers collectively
turning inward, introspective, sullen.

Finally I saw her
eyes and said, I wish you had the body you wanted,
but know I love you either way. When there's no one
to talk to in the early morning light, I
tour the landscape of your back,

mingle intoxicated in the courtyard
with white cloaked townspeople,
some of whom wear wolf masks
through the gardens and greet me
forcefully from behind.

The Patriarch

Around 3 a.m. her dreams go dark —
the gorilla quits cooing,
gets a gun,
forces her to her knees.

She does not find this funny.

When the gorilla asks her father for the money
before he blows the bitch's brains all over
the asphalt, while toddlers on tricycles
crowd the sidewalks, father responds,

would my wristwatch do instead?
It beeps every hour on the hour.

Back in bed
my thumbs squeegee her cheeks.
I shush her back to sleep.
I tell her
all this has more to do with alarm clocks
and fear of waking late for work
than with parenting.

Which may or may not be true.
Nevertheless, I'm getting new pajamas.
I've been roasting under all this fur.

A Great Mistake

I don't know about you, Jeremy said,
but I won't ever buy that brand again.
We were at the watering hole
and I wanted beef for dinner.
Jeremy was going off about what some pig said
to him at the department meeting.
He told the story, and I shook my head and licked my lips.
That didn't seem to help or ease his frustrations,
so I asked Jeremy if he and his family
wanted to go to church with me on Sunday.
He wept with the joy of 1,000 children.
Apparently, they had been trying to get invited
for quite some time. It was getting late
and, as time went on, I grew increasingly nervous
that my invitation had been a great mistake.
I was already on thin ice with the magistrate,
and if they found out about this, I would surely
be cut from the company's healthful lunch program,
which would further alienate me from Kate
in human resources, whom I love ceaselessly
and have died for many times.

On Significance

Windows down, he drives through the orange haze of perpetual afternoon. Dry heat settles on his dusty dash and will sleep there all night. The hill town quiets everything. Its hallways of ponderosa pines and squat brick buildings forever empty. Nothing like Rome, he thinks, where the cries of street vendors and dead emperors echo endlessly off marble and stone. The headlines say that yesterday an elk was spotted near the schoolhouse, and supposedly the 90-year-old wheelchair-bound war hero was bludgeoned to death when his drug deal went bad. It makes sense, he tells himself and ashes his cigarette. When he closes his eyes, a young actress calls his name. We always think there will be more time, she says. What unknowns will you regret? Her black cocktail dress melts away, revealing a pale body of heavenly frescoes — a flurry of two-dimensional angels patrol her small breasts. We always think there will be more time, she repeats. I need a whiskey, he thinks, and stops at a bar called The Snake Pit where he hopes he'll get knifed in the bathroom. Inside the place swarms with families eating ice cream, laughing endlessly in their plastic bibs.

My Friend Ben

My friend Ben knows a shit ton
about Chinese poetry. He bakes cookies
and organizes several local book clubs.
Before I go on, I should say that
there's a masked man at my back door
banging on the glass with the handle of a knife.
If you wouldn't mind notifying the authorities . . .
I must tell you that Ben plays video games
and has a website where he artfully reviews regional beers.
The best ones always remind him of his childhood summers
in rural Kansas, blue skies rolling over wheatfields.
He's reaching his hand through
the broken glass now toward the lock. I am frozen
to the couch and counting on you to alert
the police immediately. Ben's band opened
for Wilco this summer. He smokes cigarettes
sometimes while playing rhythm guitar and
knows all the guys at the guitar shop by name.
Ben's band is on the stereo now, tastefully
blending outlaw country with Kansas City jazz,
while I am being tackled into a lamp
and strangled with the cord. Certainly by now
someone has been made aware of my situation,
so I can mention to you that Ben is at the bowling alley
right now, bowling a strike like he always does
while I bleed onto my living room floor
hoping the cops don't find my good weed,
the stuff Ben grew last summer in Northern California,
an experience he rarely speaks of and barely remembers.

The Changing

Beautiful Jewish girl with big
broken heart grows weary from
so much wailing in her veins
she gorges on pianos and
decrescendos, which seems to help,
until a shaky man in red pajamas
out her closet comes
splashing everywhere
into the feeling world.

The Backyard Song

Out here in the fields,
we're always orbiting.
I orbit my wife which
is usually all right.

At the barbecue I orbit the grill,
while Terry tells jokes and my wife
laughs. Since when
have they been sleeping together?

The acid strip pressed against my cheek
floods me with Spiritus Mundi.
I see a muscular, gold god
kneel into a foamy sea.

Back in the tool shed
Terry tells me otherworldly presences
holler from his bookshelf
and frighten his children,
their brains' many colored wires.

That makes me uneasy
because Terry has no children,
so we examine the hedge
trimmers for hours.

The Unidentified Transmission

From our satellite came feelings
and radishes, a leftover
rutabaga from the Flenderson's
garden party. Something's happening.

All my friends are losing it.
Years ago, bombastic frontman
Mike Patton posed the question:
what is it? Still we don't know.

It turns people against each other.
It broke poor Julie's heart.
I woke and it found me
birthing a beautiful baby boy.

Cinque Terre

Morning fog amplifies the green hills
caught in my August morning eyes.
A gull glides, lovesick, from one hill to the other.
What is home, I wonder. The gull continues to glide.

Dotted with pink and yellow adobes,
this town we stand in rockslides down a cliff
and kisses the Ligurian Sea,
begs it not to sweep a salty arm
around the empty churches
and strong-man statues
and cover them with barnacles and slime.

I eat another strawberry and miss my wife,
who is next to me, watching pigeons
squeeze through cracks in a stone wall.
We imagine a city piled with shit and seeds

until the train arrives
and startles the birds deep into their holes
and people spill like milk from either side
and we climb in and corner an old woman

in a wheelchair who stares blankly at her feet.
Her daughter behind her barks at us to get back.

The Rutabaga

My neighbor appeared with a beer in hand.
I was on my knees pulling weeds.
The woman who used to live here
was a master gardener, he said,
and spit on the ground next to me.
A newt crawled across my gloved hand,
leaving a trail of slime. A spider soon followed.
Never a weed breached our property line,
never did a dark thought enter her brain,
take hold, and refuse to leave, my neighbor said.
Until she killed herself, I said, pointing to the garage.
That never happened, he said.
In one fluid motion,
I pulled her hacked-off head from the dirt,
stood, and began shaking it in his face.
Then explain this, I said.
That is a rutabaga, plain and simple.
I twisted the head around.
I stared into its empty sunken eyes
and began suddenly to understand;
this is a rutabaga.

The Couple Speaks of Magic

Sharma says that magic is normal
and Sam says Magic is anything but.
Could a normal person handle the ball like that?
Could a normal person get HIV

and shock the world like that?
He pulls a book from the shelf and chucks it
through the wall and into the neighbor's garage.
Well, could a normal person do such things?

He crumbles to the ground, crying.
Let me think about it, Sharma says.
She takes a drink.
Imagines a world without feet.

A world where *corn* can stand only for something delicious
and sweet. I think a normal person could, she says.
Oh, how we have lost our way, Sam bawls,
and bursts into green flame.

The children rise from their beds.
They're wearing their paper sleeping gowns.
They huddle around Sam's burning body and
murmur Magic's name.

And then one day

while driving, you rest
a Diet Coke between your thighs,
feel a strange coldness and
realize, like everything else,
the inseam of your favorite jeans
has worn away, suddenly
and blithely.

Someone bought you those jeans.
Who was she?
You see a blank face,
red hair fading to gray. There are
freckles, but they're flickering out
one by one. Once your jarred fireflies
died, who knows, who knew . . .

Bedtime Rhythm

Tom-toms open a portal. In no time
my bedroom is adrift in prairie.
The sun bleeds and swallows

the sky. A bucktoothed boy shakes
with laughter. A quail rustles near the creek;
the boy shrieks and hides beneath his mother's dress.

Dry days like these
devour everything,
even gods, she says.

Gypsies take shelter in a run-down barn
and find a primitive mask
hanging from a support beam.

Every actor is ushered
through a doorway and disappears.
Bright lights reveal the countryside.

At an all-night diner a man
hears his dead daughter's hushed cries.
He sets down his gyro and runs outside.

Looking around, the rain-soaked street
is silent and clear. He scratches his head
and returns to his seat.

For a moment he imagines her
brown bobbed hair and Easter dress.
The world is ending.

New American Eulogy

I peeked inside an urn and saw the dead thing; all these
memories of its rich life came flooding back to me!
How amazing it was to see it dead and feel
my stomach surge with primal fire; brightness blasted everything.

Nighthawks ripped through my blackened chest
to soar over starlit valleys. Even the sleepy rivers knew
I was connected to something larger than myself
and earthy scents flooded in.

Finally, freely, I wept
in the pew and during the long silent ride home.

The Father

Your eyes itch. They're tired
of being sprayed with metal shavings.
You find a melon baller. Run its edge over a flame.

First, compression. Then, an undoing.
A dripping down your nose and face.
World swells and you

wake the next weekend in a bloody bed.
Your wife is dead. A deaf toddler
keeps crying from some distant doorway.
Its corduroyed legs quiver. It signs – milk! milk! –
tiny fist pulsing.

Years ago you waded through
cornfields with a wrench. You'd climb onto giant sprinklers
twelve hours a day. The sun dared your skin
not to redden, and your skin grew a furry suit.

But how, now, can a bear assuage
this child's emptiness and fear?
When you rise, the child runs
down the hall, trips over its child feet,
slams its head through a wall, looks
back with child eyes and blames you.

Without Warning

I.

A loud man I know, but don't *really* know
or like, constantly tells me what to do.
One night he says we must get gin-drunk.
Since I am from the suburban midwest
I know not exactly what he means. Nevertheless,
I gulp down gin after gin to appease him
and be accepted by his tribe, which is,
if I am being honest, the only tribe I want to know.
One should work at all times toward honest self-examination.
Without warning, regret spreads like wildfire
through my California-shaped heart.
Though I know not what I regret, I regret intensely.
So is the way with gin, the loud man advises me.
My regret grabs onto a movie star's house
and wrestles it to the ground.
Elsewhere, my body whimpers its many sins
to a bright lime wedge that understands everything
there is to understand of human suffering.

2.

And now I'm at a bar with my real friends
and someone orders a pitcher of beer for us.
Holy shit, it's sweet. We chug and chug until we feel like kings.
Time passes and everyone's asking who ordered the pitcher,
but no one mans up. Our unease grows
to the point where someone's brow starts sweating.
It sweats so much it could be described as "sweating profusely."
And that's about all we can take
before a warlock and a warrior
emerge from a shadowy corner.
We need your help, they say.
A great village has been consumed by a darkness.
Without you that darkness could consume the whole land.
We all look at each other and are like, Fuck yeah!
Imbued with glorious purpose, we advance
to another bar and tear that shit down.

3.

It is quiet. I am alone. John Coltrane crackles,
blue and warm, from the radio. I see what he means
and pour myself some whiskey.
I watch the fire die and pour myself another.
In no time I am wearing a leather vest.
I am knifing someone in a truck stop bathroom
over and over. I throw his body to the ground —
it's me in corduroy pants, and I am smiling, and I am dead.
A snake slithers, as snakes do, from one of my many wounds.
I back against the bathroom door.
But the door is locked.
I spend 80 years reaching for that lock.

The Last Day

I walked into the bank downtown and stood in line a few minutes.
I was there to cash a check from the plasma clinic.
Eventually, a man hollered from the front door,

All right everybody. Hands up!

I turned to see a masked figure with a gun.
I shouldn't have been surprised when my right arm became a red mist,
but I was.

Oh heavens! I said.

Dammit. Sorry, said the mask. I thought the safety was on.

By then the whole place was silent except the tellers
frantically shoving bills into a paper bag.

What are you doing here? said the mask.

I came to cash my check from the plasma clinic.

Plasma clinic? Are you broke?

The recession hit me and my family harder than most.

He walked over to the tellers and grabbed a few hundred dollars.
You're working for me now. He folded and
packed the stack of bills into my breast pocket.

You really expect me to join you
in your life of crime and adventure?

Yes, he said. We've been looking for a man like you for quite some time.

He clutched the bag against his chest and backed toward the door.

Oh yeah? What kind of man is that? I said, spritzing the marble floor.

A poor family man! With only one arm!

Oh, I said. Well, in that case . . .

I followed him outside. We climbed into the getaway truck
and made for the state line.

Once I felt half safe I asked him his name.
He waited to respond, breathing heavily
behind the mask.

For now, he said, his voice hoarse
and muffled by centuries, just call me Terry.

Notes
The italicized text in "The Unruly Pond" is taken from the title of Irv Broughton's documentary about Frank Stanford.

Acknowledgements

Thanks to the editors at *BOAT*, *interrupture*, *LEVELER*, *Lilac City Fairy Tales*, *Midwestern Gothic*, *Railtown Almanac*, *Redivider*, *Strange Machine*, and *Wire Harp* for previously publishing some of these poems.

Thanks to all the generous people who donated money to the campaign to publish this book.

Special thanks to Derek Annis, Matt Furst, Keely Honeywell, Christopher Howell, Neil Legband, Tod Marshall, Simeon Mills, Kathryn Nuernberger, Curtis Perdue, Laura Read, Brent Schaeffer, Sharma Shields, Jeremy Toungate, Aileen Keown Vaux, Miles Waggener, and Maya Jewell Zeller.

Thanks most of all to Kate, forever my partner in crime and adventure.

About the Author

Tim Greenup's poems have appeared in *BOAAT*, *LEVELER*, *Midwestern Gothic*, *Redivider*, and elsewhere. He lives in Spokane with his wife and son and teaches at Spokane Falls Community College. This is his first book.